Bob Ross

A Little Golden Book® Biography

By Maria Correa

Illustrated by Jeff Crowther

For John, and our happy little life —M.C.

A GOLDEN BOOK • NEW YORK

Text copyright © 2023 by Maria Correa
Cover art and interior illustrations copyright © 2023 by Jeff Crowther
All rights reserved. Published in the United States by Golden Books, an imprint of
Random House Children's Books, a division of Penguin Random House LLC, 1745 Broadway,
New York, NY 10019. Golden Books, A Golden Book, A Little Golden Book, the G colophon,
and the distinctive gold spine are registered trademarks of Penguin Random House LLC.
rhcbooks.com
Educators and librarians, for a variety of teaching tools, visit us at RHTeachersLibrarians.com
Library of Congress Control Number: 2022931975
ISBN 978-0-593-56825-5 (trade) — ISBN 978-0-593-56826-2 (ebook)
Printed in the United States of America
10 9 8 7 6

*R*obert Norman Ross was born on October 29, 1942, in Daytona Beach, Florida. His mother, Ollie, taught him to love and respect wildlife. Bob learned that to make friends with trees, all he had to do was talk to them.

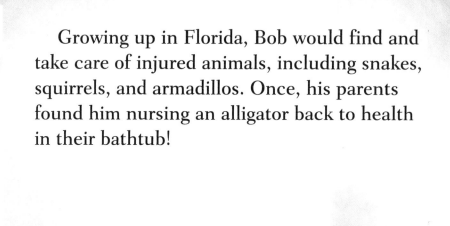

Growing up in Florida, Bob would find and take care of injured animals, including snakes, squirrels, and armadillos. Once, his parents found him nursing an alligator back to health in their bathtub!

Bob's father, Jack, was a carpenter. When Bob was in ninth grade, he decided to quit school and train to be a carpenter, too. While working with his father, Bob lost the tip of his left index finger in an accident.

Bob decided that woodworking wasn't for him. He joined the United States Air Force when he was eighteen, and shortly afterward was sent to live on a base in Alaska.

Alaska's dramatic landscapes and snowcapped mountains were unlike anything Bob had seen before.

Inspired by his surroundings, Bob took his first painting class in Alaska. Though he enjoyed painting, he was frustrated by his teachers, who preferred abstract art to realism. Bob wanted to learn how to paint a tree that actually looked like a tree!

One day while watching TV, Bob discovered a
show called *The Magic of Oil Painting*. The host,
a German painter named William Alexander (who
lived in Bob's home state of Florida), completed a
landscape painting during each thirty-minute episode
while explaining his technique. Bob was fascinated.

Bill Alexander used an oil painting technique called alla prima, or "the first attempt" in Italian. Also known as wet-on-wet, this approach allows artists to finish paintings quickly by applying new layers of paint without waiting for previous layers to dry.

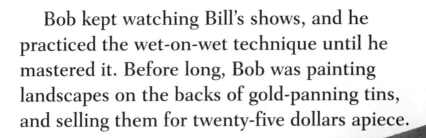

Bob kept watching Bill's shows, and he practiced the wet-on-wet technique until he mastered it. Before long, Bob was painting landscapes on the backs of gold-panning tins, and selling them for twenty-five dollars apiece.

In 1981, Bob retired from the air force as a master sergeant and moved back to Florida to study in person with Bill Alexander. Bob even joined Bill's company as a traveling instructor.

In one of Bob's painting workshops, he met Annette Kowalski. Annette saw his talent and knew he could be a big success.

Annette and her husband became Bob's business partners. Together with Bob's wife, Jane, they started Bob Ross Inc., launching a line of paints and brushes.

Although Bob's hair was naturally straight, he saved money on haircuts by getting a perm, a curly hairstyle that can last a long time. He didn't really like the look, but it became the company's logo, so he never changed it.

At first, the company struggled. Bob's shopping-mall painting classes attracted only small audiences. Annette bought local newspaper ads, and even set up a telephone hotline to generate buzz. Eventually, their big break came in the form of a TV show.

The Joy of Painting first aired on January 11, 1983, on PBS. Over the next eleven years, Bob would film 403 episodes. In each, he stood in a dark room with a blank canvas. With a smudge here and a palette-knife scrape there, he'd bring an imaginary landscape scene to life in half an hour.

But *The Joy of Painting* wasn't just about the masterpieces Bob created—it was about sharing the experience with his viewers. He believed that anyone could be an artist and that art should be accessible to everyone. On his show, he used just thirteen paint colors and only a handful of tools.

Alizarin Crimson

Bright Red

Indian Yellow

Phthalo Blue

Van Dyke Brown

Sap Green

Yellow Ochre

Dark Sienna

Phthalo Green

Cadmium Yellow

Prussian Blue

Midnight Black

Like Bill Alexander, Bob explained his process step-by-step so that viewers could paint along with him. But many people tuned in simply to watch Bob and to listen to his calm, soothing voice as he painted his "happy little trees."

script liner: used for fine details, like twigs

fan brush: ideal for making forests

2-inch brush: perfect for painting skies and trees

Titanium white

Palette knife: great for forming mighty mountains and riverbanks

Bob remained an animal lover his entire life. Occasionally, animals that Bob was helping to rehabilitate appeared on his show. These included a baby raccoon, a fawn, an owl named Hoot, and—perhaps the most famous of all—Peapod the squirrel.

The Joy of Painting is considered to be the most popular art show in history. People from all over the country—and the world—turned on their televisions and turned to Bob for inspiration.

Bob died on July 4, 1995, but his legacy lives on. Today there are more than 3,000 official Bob Ross instructors worldwide. And although he never received recognition from the art world during his lifetime, you can now find some of his paintings in the Smithsonian's National Museum of American History's permanent collection.

Bob Ross didn't just teach people how to paint. He taught people to *believe* they could paint. So the next time you need a little encouragement, just think of Bob's friendly voice saying, "You can move mountains. You can do anything."